OTHER BOOKS IN THIS SERIES:
"Dance is the air we breathe" – Dance Quotations
"Sing your song looking up at the sky" – Opera Quotation

Dedicated to my mother, Marion Garretty – who taught me to love books.
And to Frederick Fitzwalter-Read, her pop, who taught her that with books
to read, you're never lonely.

Front cover quotation by Charles W. Eliot (1834-1926)

Published in Great Britain in 1991 by Exley Publications Ltd.
First published in the USA in 1992 by Exley Giftbooks.

12   11   10   9   8   7   6   5   4   3   2

Copyright © Helen Exley 1991
The moral right of the author has been asserted.

ISBN 1-86187-517-7

Picture research by Alexander Goldberg. Printed in China.

Exley Publications Ltd, 16 Chalk Hill, Watford, Herts WD19 4BG, UK.
Exley Publications LLC, 185 Main Street, Spencer MA 01562, USA.
www.helenexleygiftbooks.com

Acknowledgements: PAMELA BROWN, HELEN EXLEY, MARION C. GARRETTY, CHARLOTTE
GRAY, MAYA V. PATEL, HELEN THOMSON, JENNY DE VRIES: published with permission ©
Helen Exley 1991. Picture credits: Cover and P. 50, Carl Spitzweg, "Der Bucherwurm", Archiv Fur
Kunst; P. 5, Gustav Cederstrom, "An Interior With A Woman Reading By A Table", Christie's Colour
Library; P. 7, Hans Heyerdahl, "At The Window", Nasjonalgallereit, Oslo, Bridgeman Art Library; P. 8
Maestro dell Annunciazione, Scala; P. 10, Codice, Biblioteca Trivulziana, Milan, Scala; P. 13 (and Bac
Cover), Sir Lawrence Alma-Tadema, "Ninety-four Degrees In The Shade", © Fitzwilliam Museum; P.
14, Evert Collier, detail from "Vanitas With Musical Instruments, Books and Globes", Bridgeman Art
Library; P. 17, Elizabeth Adela Stanhope Forbes, "Idle Moments", Christie's Colour Library; P. 18,
Gwen John "Le Saint Livre", private collection, Edimedia; P. 21, Sandra McCabe, "Quiet Lawn",
Montague Ward; P. 22, Perronneau Jean Baptiste, "Ragazzo con Libro", Hermitage Museum,
Leningrad, Scala; P. 24, Carl Larsson, "Portrait of Dora Lamm", Christie's Colour Library; P. 27,
Christie's Colour Library; P. 28, Oscar Bluhm, Christie's Colour Library; P. 31, Wilhelm Steinhausen,
"Portraet", Staatliche Kunsthalle, Karlsruhe, Archiv Fur Kunst; P. 33, Scaffali con Libri, Museo
Bibliografico Musicale, Bologna, Scala; P. 34, Henry Ottmann "Woman on a Balcony", Musee des
Beaux-Arts, Rouen, The Bridgeman Art Library; P. 37, Valdemar Kornerup, "Reading To Mother",
Christie's Colour Library; P. 38, B. Pothast, "A Good Story", Christie's Colour Library; P. 40, Jean
Pucelle "Brevarie", Bibliteque National, Paris, Scala; P. 42, Antoni Vila Arrufat, "A Girl Reading",
Museo de Arte, Sabadell, Barcelona, The Bridgeman Art Library; P. 44, Edouard Manet, "Emile Zola"
Musee du Louvre, Archiv Fur Kunst; P. 47, "Girl Reading", Christie's Colour Library; P. 48;
Colantonio, Museo di Capodimonte, Scala; P. 52, Alois Priechenfald, detail from "Studying The
Talmud", Christie's Colour Library; P. 55, Carl Spitzweg, "Ein Besuch", Archiv Fur Kunst; P. 56, "The
Book-Burning", Scala; P. 59,Paul Fischer, "The Afternoon Read", Christie's Colour Library; P. 61, Sir
John Lavery, "Girl In A Red Dress Seated By A Swimming Pool", Christie's Colour Library.

"Books...
the quietest and most constant of friends"

BOOK LOVERS QUOTATIONS

A HELEN EXLEY GIFTBOOK

"There is more treasure in books than in all the pirates' loot on Treasure Island... and best of all, you can enjoy these riches every day of your life."
WALT DISNEY (1901 - 66)

.Q.

"Only one hour in the normal day is more pleasurable than the hour spent in bed with a book before going to sleep, and that is the hour spent in bed with a book after being called in the morning."
ROSE MACAULAY (1881 - 1958)

.Q.

"Just the knowledge that a good book is waiting one at the end of a long day makes that day happier."
KATHLEEN NORRIS (1880 - 1966)

.Q.

"They [books] support us in solitude.... They help us to forget the coarseness of men and things, compose our cares and our passions, and lay our disappointments to sleep."
STEPHANIE FÉLICITÉ GENLIS (1746 - 1830),
from *Memoires*

.Q.

"Sometimes when I can't go to sleep at night I see the family of the future. Dressed in three-tone shorts-and-shirt sets of disposable Papersilk, they sit before the television wall of their apartment, only their eyes moving. After I've looked a while I always see - otherwise I'd die - a pigheaded soul over in the corner with a book; only his eyes are moving, but in them there is a different look."

RANDALL JARRELL

"We have entered a world of shorthand, precis, digest, summary, news flash, comic strip. We are bombarded with visual images, cutting from one to another, stabbing at the mind and put out with the rubbish sacks at the end of the week.

The novel that took a man or woman years to create - in research, in the planning of the plot and counter-plot, in construction - each word chosen, each phrase weighed against another, themes recurring, climaxes achieved - is now reduced to a four part serial, produced with pride in the accuracy of its sets and costumes, brilliantly acted, the music of the background authentic to the period. The words, but not the minds. The science, but not the significance.

The book has been made a thing to watch, not to live. We must fight to save the written word as we fight to save the whale. We must keep in our minds a place apart, a sanctuary, where a lamp lights only the table at which we sit, where the curtains are drawn against the present time. Let us begin."

PAMELA BROWN, b.1928

·Ω·

"Books - what they make a movie out of for television."

LEONARD LOUIS LEVINSON

·Ω·

CODICE, BIBLIOTECA TRIVULZIANA

"In books lie the soul of the whole Past Time; the articulate audible voice of the Past, when the body and material substances of it has altogether vanished like a dream."
THOMAS CARLYLE (1795 - 1881),
from *The Hero as Man of Letters*.

.Q.

"The reading of all good books is like a conversation with the finest men of past centuries."
RENÉ DESCARTES (1596 - 1650)

.Q.

"Literature transmits incontroversial condensed experience from generation to generation. In this way literature becomes the living memory of a nation."
ALEXANDER SOLZHENITSYN (b.1918)

.Q.

"The worst thing about new books is that they keep us from reading old ones."
JOSEPH JOUBERT (1754 - 1824)

.Q.

"A book is the only place in which you can examine a fragile thought without breaking it, or explore an explosive idea without fear it will go off in your face.... It is one of the few havens remaining where [your] mind can get both provocation and privacy."
EDWARD P. MORGAN

·Q·

"Some books are to be tasted, others to be swallowed, and some few to be chewed and digested; that is, some books are to be read only in parts; others to be read but not curiously; and some few to be read wholly, and with diligence and attention."
FRANCIS BACON (1561 - 1626)

·Q·

"When you read a classic you do not see in the book more than you did before. You see more in *you* than there was before."
CLIFTON FADIMAN
(American essayist)

·Q·

"NINETY-FOUR DEGREES IN THE SHADE"
BY SIR LAWRENCE ALMA-TADEMA ▷

"A great writer is, so to speak, a second government in his country. And for that reason no regime has ever loved great writers, only minor ones."
ALEXANDER SOLZHENITSYN b.1918

"... it is not without reason that writers in our country are called engineers of the human soul."
NIKITA KHRUSHCHEV (1894 - 1971)

"To read too many books is harmful."
MAO TSE-TUNG (1893 - 1976)

"Books differ from all other propaganda media, primarily because one single book can significantly change the reader's attitude and action to an extent unmatched by the impact of any other single medium."

A member of the CIA's Covert Action Staff,
from *Foreign and Military Intelligence, Book One*

.Ọ.

"Literature, fiction, poetry, whatever, makes justice in the world. That's why it almost always has to be on the side of the underdog."

GRACE PALEY
(American writer)

.Ọ.

"Books can be dangerous. The best ones should be labelled 'This could change your life'."

HELEN EXLEY

.Ọ.

"Beneath the rule of men entirely great,
The pen is mightier than the sword."

EDWARD BULWER-LYTTON (1803 - 73)
(British novelist and politician)

.Ọ.

"Words have a power beyond their meaning.
I remember the stories of my childhood, but I remember
the single words that shone out of fairy stories - milk
and buns, a flask of wine, a cabbage cut fresh from the
garden. I see the whiteness, feel the sticky brown,
marvel at the beads of moisture on thin, cold glass, hear
the knife click through the stem and touch the dew
along the ribbed leaves. I would read again stories that
frightened me, for the sake of such perceptions. They
seem to echo an older life, beyond my knowing."
PAMELA BROWN, 1928

.Q.

"There is a space on everyone's bookshelves for books
one has outgrown but cannot give away. They hold
one's youth between their leaves, like flowers pressed on
a half-forgotten summer's day."
MARION C. GARRETTY, b.1917

.Q.

"I am part of all that I have read."
JOHN KIERAN

.Q.

" 'And what are you reading, Miss -?' 'Oh! it is only a
novel!' replies the young lady: while she lays down her
book with affected indifference, or momentary shame.
'It is only Cecilia, or Camilla, or Belinda:' or, in short,
only some work in which the most thorough knowledge
of human nature, the happiest delineation of its
varieties, the liveliest effusions of wit and humour are
conveyed to the world in the best chosen language."
JANE AUSTEN (1775 - 1817)
from *Northanger Abbey*

.Q.

"In my opinion the readers of novels are far more
intelligent than unsuccessful writers will believe. They
are expert in detecting and merciless to the conceited
author, and the insincere author, and the author with
all the tools of literature at his command who has
nothing to say worth reading."
NEVIL SHUTE

.Q.

"A man ought to read just as inclination leads him; for
what he reads as a task will do him little good."
SAMUEL JOHNSON (1709 - 84)

"The wonderful thing about libraries and bookstores - even the television or the radio - is that no one is forcing you to read anything, or to go to any particular movie, or to watch something on television or listen to something on the radio. You have free choice."
JUDITH KRUG
the American Library Association

.Ω.

"The way a book is read - which is to say, the qualities a reader brings to a book - can have as much to do with its worth as anything the author puts into it...Anyone who can read can learn how to read deeply and thus live more fully."
NORMAN COUSINS

.Ω.

"It is only by the love of reading that the evil resulting from the association with little minds can be counteracted."
ELIZABETH HAMILTON

.Ω.

"RAGAZZO CON LIBRO" BY PERRONNEAU JEAN BAPTISTE

"**My** education was the liberty I had to read indiscriminately and all the time, with my eyes hanging out."
DYLAN THOMAS (1914 - 53)
(Welsh poet)

.Q.

"I know exactly how I felt when I first read *The Brothers Karamazov*. I can still taste the words, smell the air of a Russian winter."
HELEN THOMSON, b.1943

.Q.

"Books are the quietest and most constant of friends; they are the most accessible and wisest of counsellors, and the most patient of teachers."
CHARLES W. ELIOT (1834 - 1926)
(Educator)

.Q.

"A classic is a book that has never finished saying what it has to say."
ITALO CALVINO, b.1923
(Italian writer)

.Q.

"Some books are undeservedly forgotten; none are undeservedly remembered."
W.H. AUDEN (1907 - 1973)
(British poet)

.Ω.

"There can hardly be a stranger commodity in the world than books. Printed by people who don't understand them; sold by people who don't understand them; bound, criticized and read by people who don't understand them; and now even written by people who don't understand them."
GEORG CHRISTOPH LICHTENBERG

.Ω.

"Education... has produced a vast population able to read but unable to distinguish what is worth reading."
GEORGE MACAULAY TREVELYAN (1876 - 1962)

.Ω.

"The ratio of literacy to illiteracy is constant, but nowadays the illiterates can read."
ALBERTO MORAVIA, b.1907
(Italian writer)

.Ω.

"The true University of these days is a collection of books."
THOMAS CARLYLE (1795 - 1881)

.Q.

"Books are the main source of our knowledge, our reservoir of faith, memory, wisdom, morality, poetry, philosophy, history and science."
DANIEL J. BOORSTIN,
from the report *Books in our Future*

.Q.

"All that Mankind has done, thought, gained or been: it is lying as in magic preservation in the pages of books. They are the chosen possession of man."
THOMAS CARLYLE (1795 - 1881)

.Q.

"Books are the carriers of civilization."
BARBARA TUCHMAN, b.1912
(American historian)

.Q.

"ARAB SCHOLARS"

"There is a great deal of solemn discussion about The Novel. In fact, every novel is an answer to the ancient plea, 'Tell us a story'."
PAMELA BROWN, 1928

.Ω.

"Nothing very much happens in her books, and yet, when you come to the bottom of a page, you eagerly turn it to learn what will happen next. Nothing very much does and again you eagerly turn the page. The novelist who has the power to achieve this has the most precious gift a novelist can possess."
W. SOMERSET MAUGHAM (1874 - 1965)
British novelist, referring to Jane Austen

.Ω.

"We settle to read any work of fiction with the same squirm of anticipation primitive people experienced as they gathered closer to the fire and the storyteller began the tale."
JENNY DE VRIES

.Ω.

"**D**ear Mr. and Mrs. Younis:
I wish you great success in banning the book *Boss* from
your local high school. And I offer my support.
It is a filthy sex perverted book, filled with shocking
language and scenes too horrible to mention. Why, it
would probably make Harold Robbins blush.
I hope that erotic, unspeakable book is banned before
the birthrate in your town soars.
By the way - I have another book on the market right
now. If there's anything you can do about getting that
one banned, too, I'd really appreciate it."
MIKE ROYKO'S response to attempts to ban his book, *Boss*.

.Ω.

"Censorship always defeats it own purpose, for it creates
in the end the kind of society that is incapable of
exercising real discretion."
HENRY STEELE COMMAGER
(Historian)

.Ω.

"The burning of an author's books, imprisonment for
opinion's sake, has always been the tribute that an
ignorant age pays to the genius of its time."
JOSEPH LEWIS

.Ω.

"PORTRAET", BY WILHELM STEINHAUSEN

"When I get a little money, I buy books; and if any is left, I buy food and clothes."
DESIDERIUS ERASMUS (1465 - 1536)

.Ọ.

"Sir, the fact that a book is in the public library brings no comfort. Books are the one element in which I am personally and nakedly acquisitive. If it weren't for the law I would steal them. If it weren't for my purse I would buy them."
HAROLD LASKI (1893 - 1950)

.Ọ.

"The organized soul has one book beside the bed. The glutton sleeps with a New York skyline lurching an inch from the bed."
CHARLOTTE GRAY, b.1937
(British poet)

.Ọ.

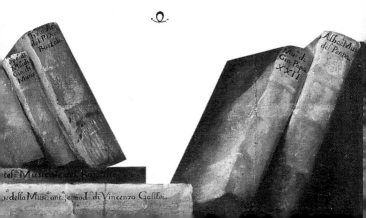

"No entertainment is so cheap as reading, nor any
pleasure so lasting."
MARY WORTLEY MONTAGU (1689 - 1762)

.Ω.

"There is little in life to equal finding a book long
sought and long out of print."
DR. MAYA V. PATEL, b.1943

.Ω.

"There's something special about people who are
interested in the printed word. They are a species all
their own - learned, kind, knowledgeable and human."
NATHAN PINE
(Bookseller)

.Ω.

"Literary fiction, whether directed to the purpose of transient amusement, or adopted as an indirect medium of instruction, has always in its most genuine form exhibited a mirror of the times in which it is composed; reflecting morals, customs, manners, peculiarity of character, and prevalence of opinion. Thus, perhaps, after all, it forms the best history of nations..."
SYDNEY OWENSON MORGAN, 1813

.Q.

"The novel's essence is complexity. Every novel says to the reader 'Things are not as simple as you think'. That is the novel's eternal truth, but its voice grows ever fainter in a world based on easy quick answers that come before and rule out the question."
MILAN KUNDERA
(Czech writer)

.Q.

"All books are divisible into two classes; the book of the hour and the books of all time."
JOHN RUSKIN (1819 - 1900)

.Q.

"We rely upon the poets, the philosophers, and the playwrights to articulate what most of us can only feel, in joy or sorrow. They illuminate the thoughts for which we only grope; they give us the strength and balm we cannot find in ourselves.
Whenever I feel my courage wavering I rush to them. They give me the wisdom of acceptance, the will and resilience to push on."
HELEN HAYES

⟡

"That is part of the beauty of all literature. You discover that your longings are universal longings, that you're not lonely and isolated from anyone.
You belong."
F. SCOTT FITZGERALD (1896 - 1940)

⟡

"Literature is my Utopia. Here I am not disenfranchised. No barrier of the senses shuts me out from the sweet, gracious discourse of my book friends. They talk to me without embarrassment or awkwardness."
HELEN KELLER

⟡

"READING TO MOTHER", BY VALDEMAR KORNERUP

"A GOOD STORY", BY B. POTHAST

"For children, the joy of a book is not merely the story but the feel, the taste, the smell of it - the texture of the paper, the size and shape of the typeface, the illustrations, flaws, marks, even the numbering of the pages.

My *Peter Pan* was the cheapest of editions, with an indented Mabel Lucy Atwell Peter on the red cover. The paper was thick, the illustration line drawings set into the text. I still know that little book as if I held it in my hands. The memory holds the cold air of my bedroom, the nightlight in its saucer, the car lights crossing the ceiling, my father's voice."

PAMELA BROWN, b. 1928

.Q.

"When I was a ten-year-old book worm and used to kiss the dust jacket pictures of authors as if they were icons, it used to amaze me that these remote people could provoke me to love."

ERICA JONG, b.1942

.Q.

dicius. fera. iiij. Inuitatorium.	non fuit timor
In manu tua domine omnes	Quoniam deus dissipauit
fines terre. ant'. Euerte. ps' dd'	ossa eorum: qui hominibus
	placent: confusi sunt quoniam

xit insipiens in corde
suo: non est deus
Corrupti sunt et ab hominibus
viles facti sunt in iniquitatibus:
non est qui faciat bonum
Deus de celo prospicit super fi-
lios hominum: ut videat si est
intelligens aut requirens deum
Omnes declinauerunt z si-
mul inutiles facti sunt: non
est qui faciat bonum non est
usque ad unum
Nonne scient omnes qui o-
perantur iniquitatem: qui
deuorant plebem meam ut ci-
bum panis
Deum non inuocauerunt:
illic trepidauerunt timore ubi

non fuit timor
Quoniam deus dissipauit
ossa eorum: qui hominibus
placent: confusi sunt quoniam
deus spreuit eos
Quis dabit ex syon salutare
israel: cum conuerterit dominus captiuitatem plebis sue:
exultabit iacob et letabitur
israel. psalmus dauid
Deus in nomine tuo sal-
uum me fac: et in vir-
tute tua iudica me
Deus exaudi orationem me-
am: auribus percipe verba oris
mei
Quoniam alieni insurre-
xerunt aduersum me et fortes
quesierunt animam meam:
et non proposuerunt deum
ante conspectum suum
Ecce enim deus adiuuat
me: et dominus susceptor est
anime mee
Auerte mala inimicis me-
is: in veritate tua disperde illos
Voluntarie sacrificabo tibi:
et confitebor nomini tuo domine
quoniam bonum est
Quoniam ex omni tribula

"Certain books have exerted a profound influence on history, culture, civilization and scientific thought throughout recorded time.... In every historical era, we find overwhelming evidence of the power of the written word, without which a high state of civilization and culture is inconceivable in any time or place."
ROBERT B. DOWNS, from *Books That Changed The World*

.Ω.

"If anyone has any doubt about the importance of books, or about the adage that the pen is mightier than the sword, it's worth considering that Plato's *Republic*, the Bible, the Koran, Darwin's *Origin of Species*, Marx's *Das Kapital*, Hitler's *Mein Kampf*, and *The Thoughts of Mao Tse-tung* have probably changed the course of history as much as any process or event, any individual or any nation."
AUTHOR UNKNOWN

.Ω.

"Poets are the unacknowledged legislators of the world."
PERCY BYSSHE SHELLEY (1792 - 1822)

.Ω.

"Books are keys to wisdom's treasure;
Books are gates to lands of pleasure;
Books are paths that upward lead;
Books are friends. Come, let us read."
EMILIE POULSSON,
inscription in Children's Reading Room, Hopkington, Massachusetts

.Ọ.

"It is a great thing to start life with a small number of
really good books which are your very own."
SHERLOCK HOLMES

.Ọ.

"When you read to a child, when you put a book in a
child's hands, you are bringing that child news of the
infinitely varied nature of life. You are an awakener."
PAULA FOX
(American author)

.Ọ.

"The dirtiest book of all is an expurgated book."
WALT WHITMAN (1819 - 92)

.Q.

"It is absurd to have a hard-and-fast rule about what
one should read and what one shouldn't.
More than half of modern culture depends on
what one shouldn't read."
OSCAR WILDE (1854 - 1900)

.Q.

"This pictorial account of the day-to-day life of an
English gamekeeper is full of considerable interest to
outdoor minded readers, as it contains many passages
on pheasant-raising, the apprehending of poachers, ways
to control vermin, and other chores and duties of the
professional gamekeeper.
Unfortunately, one is obliged to wade through many
pages of extraneous material in order to discover and
savour those sidelights on the management of a midland
shooting estate, and in this reviewer's opinion the book
cannot take the place of J.R. Miller's
Practical Gamekeeping."
A review of *Lady Chatterley's Lover* in *Field and Stream*

.Q.

◁ "EMILE ZOLA" BY MANET

"**I**n a very real sense, people who have read good
literature have lived more than people who cannot or
will not read... It is not true that we have only one life to
live; if we can read, we can live as many more lives and
as many kinds of lives as we wish."
S. I. HAYAKAWA

.ꙮ.

"A novel is the chance to try on a
different life for size."
MARION C. GARRETTY, b.1917

.ꙮ.

"Dreams, books, are each a world, and books we know,
Are a substantial world, both pure and good.
Round these, with tendrils strong as flesh and blood,
Our pastime and our happiness will grow."
WILLIAM WORDSWORTH (1770 - 1850),
from *Personal Talk*

.ꙮ.

"Too many people in the modern world view poetry
as a luxury, not a necessity like petrol.
But to me it's the oil of life."
SIR JOHN BETJEMAN (1906 - 84)

"These are not books, lumps of lifeless paper, but *minds* alive on the shelves. From each of them goes out its own voice... and just as the touch of a button on our set will fill the room with music, so by taking down one of these volumes and opening it, one can call into range the voice of a person far distant in time and space, and hear them speaking to us, mind to mind, heart to heart."

GILBERT HIGHET

.𝒬.

"Books are a delightful society. If you go into a room filled with books, even without taking them down from their shelves, they seem to speak to you, to welcome you."

WILLIAM E. GLADSTONE (1809 - 98)

.𝒬.

"Books become as familiar and necessary as old friends. Each change in them, brought about by much handling and by accident only endears them more. They are an extension of oneself."

CHARLOTTE GRAY

.𝒬.

"If you cannot read all your books, at any rate handle, or as it were, fondle them - peer into them, let them fall open where they will, read from the first sentence that arrests the eye, set them back on the shelves with your own hands, arrange them on your own plan so that you at least know where they are. Let them be your friends; let them at any rate be your acquaintances."
WINSTON CHURCHILL (1874 - 1965)

.Q.

"It should be possible to exist with only a short shelf of books, to read and give away. After all - we may not open a book, once read, for ten years or more.
But the act of reading has made it part of us - to relinquish it would be to lose an extension of being."
PAM BROWN, b.1928
(British author)

.Q.

"Books, books, books. It was not that I read so much. I read and re-read the same ones. But all of them were necessary to me. Their presence, their smell, the letters of their titles, and the texture of their leather bindings."
COLETTE (1873 - 1954)
(French writer)

.Q.

DETAIL FROM "STUDYING THE TALMUD"

"For books are more than books, they are the life
The very heart and core of ages past,
The reason why men lived and worked and died,
The essence and quintessence of their lives."
AMY LOWELL (1874 - 1925)

.♀.

"Books are a form of immortality. The words of people
whose bodies are dust still live in their books....
All the great lives that have lived have been told
about in books."
WILFRED A. PETERSON,
from *The Art of Living by Day*

.♀.

"In books we have the compendium of all human
experience. We may use them or neglect them as we
will, but if we use them, we may share the courage and
endurance of adventurers, the thoughts of sages, the
vision of poets and the raptures of lovers, and - some
few of us perhaps - the ecstasies of Saints."
SIR BASIL BLACKWELL

.♀.

"One of the delights of being older is being able to control ideas. I have suffered all my life from disease called Brains in the Head... In youth you keep bubbling with ideas. They may be foolish but you can't stop them. I've now learnt not to suffer too much from the Brains... As you get older your judgement develops. One of my joys is having my mind stirred by a good book, and not feeling I've got to go to the typewriter afterwards. There is nothing nicer than nodding off while reading. Going fast asleep then being woken up by the crash of the book on the floor, then saying to yourself, well it doesn't matter much. An admirable feeling."

A. J. P. TAYLOR
(British Historian)
from an interview in the *Evening Standard*, March 1982

.Ọ.

"No book is really worth reading at the age of ten which is not equally (and often far more) worth reading at the age of fifty and beyond."

C.S. LEWIS (1898 - 1963)

.Ọ.

"EIN BESUCH" BY CARL SPITZWEG

"THE BOOK-BURNING"

"We all know that books burn - yet we have the greater knowledge that books cannot be killed by fire. People die, but books never die. No man and no force can abolish memory... In this war, we know, books are weapons."
FRANKLIN D. ROOSEVELT

.Ѻ.

"Censorship is the younger of two ugly sisters; the name of the other is Inquisition."
LUDWIG BORNE

.Ѻ.

"Whenever they burn books they will also, in the end, burn human beings."
HEINRICH HEINE
(German poet/philosopher)

.Ѻ.

"The books that the world calls immoral are books that show the world its shame."
OSCAR WILDE (1854 - 1900)

.Ѻ.

"**A** moment ago it was the depth of winter, the desolate moors stretching away into the snowy dark. Now, abruptly, there is sunlight, the smell of summer, the familiar room.
The book lies on your knees. Closed.
The story is done."
PAMELA BROWN, b.1928
(British author)

.Ω.

"If I read a book that impresses me, I have to take myself firmly in hand before I mix with other people; otherwise they would think my mind rather queer."
ANNE FRANK (1929 - 45)

.Ω.

"It is very difficult for a man who has fallen in love with Rosalind and Heloise, Emma and the Duchess of Malfi, to settle for someone merely alive.
And where is a woman to find a Sir Lancelot?"
MAYA V. PATEL

.Ω.

"THE AFTERNOON READ", BY PAUL FISCHER

"**M**y best friends have all been dead two hundred years or more. Jane, Sam Johnson and Sam Pepys, Bede and Julian of Norwich, Herodatus, Xenophon. Dear friends I cannot quite believe I've never met."
PAMELA BROWN, b. 1928

.Ω.

"A good book is the best of friends, the same to-day and for ever."
MARTIN FARQUHAR TUPPER (1810 - 89)

.Ω.

"The first time I read an excellent book, it is to me just as if I had gained a new friend: when I read over a book I have perused before, it resembles the meeting with an old one."
OLIVER GOLDSMITH (1728 - 74)

.Ω.

"Finishing a good book is like leaving a good friend."
WILLIAM FEATHER
(American businessman)

.Ω.